ASTRONAUT TRAVEL GUIDES

THE MOON

CHRIS OXLADE

Raintree

www.raintreepublishers.co.uk
Visit our website to find out
more information about
Raintree books.

To order:
☎ Phone 0845 6044371
🖷 Fax +44 (0) 1865 312263
✉ Email myorders@raintreepublishers.co.uk

Customers from outside the UK please telephone +44 1865 312262

Raintree is an imprint of Capstone Global Library
Limited, a company incorporated in England and
Wales having its registered office at 7 Pilgrim
Street, London, EC4V 6LB – Registered company
number: 6695582

Text © Capstone Global Library Limited 2013
First published in hardback in 2013
First published in paperback in 2014
The moral rights of the proprietor have been
asserted.

Edited by Nancy Dickmann and Laura Knowles
Designed by Steve Mead
Illustration on p. 21 by Jeff Edwards
Original illustrations © Capstone Global
   Library Ltd 2013
Picture research by Mica Brancic
Originated by Capstone Global Library Ltd
Printed and bound in China by CTPS

ISBN 978 1 406 23976 8 (hardback)
16 15 14 13 12
10 9 8 7 6 5 4 3 2 1

ISBN 978 1 406 23986 7 (paperback)
17 16 15 14 13
10 9 8 7 6 5 4 3 2 1

British Library Cataloguing in Publication Data
Oxlade, Chris.
The Moon. – (Astronaut travel guides)
523.3-dc23
A full catalogue record for this book is available
from the British Library.

Acknowledgements
We would like to thank the following for
permission to reproduce photographs: Corbis
pp. 8 (© Bettmann), 7 (© Sunset Boulevard),
ESA p. 5 bottom and 18 (NASA); © ESA-CNES-
ARIANESPACE p. 27 (Optique Vidéo du CSG/JM
Guillon); John Spencer p. 34; NASA pp. 4 (JPL),
5 middle and 30 (Johnson Space Center), 5 top
and 17 (Headquarters), 11 (Ames Research
Center/Northrup Grumman), 16 (Johnson Space
Center), 20 (Johnson Space Center), 22 (Johnson
Space Center), 23 (Johnson Space Center), 25
(Johnson Space Center), 26 (Johnson Space
Center), 28, 29, 37, 38. Science Photo Library
pp. 9 (Omikron), 10 (Detlev Van Ravenswaay),
12 (NASA), 15 (Eckhard Slawik), 31 (NASA);
Shutterstock pp. 32 (© Ismael Jorda), 40-41
(© Martiin/Fluidworkshop).

Design image elements reproduced with
permission of Shutterstock/© Diego Barucco/
© Rafael Pacheco/© Reistlin Magere.

Cover photograph of the Earth and Moon
reproduced with permission of Shutterstock/
© Ibooo7.

We would like to thank John Spencer, Paolo
Nespoli, and ESA for their invaluable help in the
preparation of this book.

Every effort has been made to contact copyright
holders of material reproduced in this book.
Any omissions will be rectified in subsequent
printings if notice is given to the publisher.

CONTENTS

Some words are shown in bold, **like this**. You can find out what they mean by looking in the glossary.

DON'T FORGET

These boxes will remind you what you need to take with you on your big adventure.

NUMBER CRUNCHING

Don't miss these little chunks of data as you whizz through the travel guide!

AMAZING FACTS

You need to know these fascinating facts to get the most out of your space safari!

WHO'S WHO?

Find out about the space explorers who have studied the Universe in the past and today.

DESTINATION MOON

How often have you looked up at the Moon in the night sky? Have you looked through a **telescope** to see its surface covered with **craters**? The Moon is our closest neighbour in space, and it's the only object in space that astronauts have visited. Have you wondered what it would be like to visit the Moon? This is the place to find out!

Looking at the Moon from Earth through a small telescope or large binoculars reveals a world littered with deep craters and dark patches called seas.

WHY VISIT THE MOON?

There are plenty of good reasons to visit the Moon. For a start, you can find out about Moon rocks and what's inside the Moon. This can help us to learn about how the Earth was formed. You can also look for places to build a Moon base, from where we could launch a mission to Mars in the future.

The Moon is simply an amazing place to visit. Things to see on the **lunar** surface include giant craters, vast flat "seas" of frozen **lava**, mountains, and **canyons**. Just imagine walking across the dusty surface of the Moon, and looking up to see Earth in the sky. Only 12 people have ever stood on the Moon. Could you be the next?

Turn to page 17 to find out what to expect when you take your first steps on the Moon.

Get tips on what to pack for your journey on pages 30–31.

Discover what life is like in space from astronaut Paolo Nespoli on page 18.

AMAZING FACTS

No country owns the Moon, or any part of the Moon. So no need to take a passport! The Outer Space Treaty is an international agreement made in 1967 that says no country can claim the Moon as its own, and that the Moon can only be used for peaceful purposes.

THE MOON IN HISTORY

Humans must have looked up at the Moon for hundreds of thousands of years. But until telescopes were invented in the 1600s, people knew little about its surface. Today, we know a lot more. In more modern times, scientists have carefully mapped the Moon, and sent **probes** to visit it. Astronauts have even landed there.

WHO'S WHO?

In ancient times, the people of many different cultures had gods and goddesses associated with the Moon.

GOD OR GODDESS	PLACE WORSHIPPED
Khons	Ancient Egypt
Artemis	Ancient Greece
Diana	Ancient Rome
Selena or Luna	Ancient Greece
Chandra	India
Heng-O	China
Ix Chel	Central America
Mawu	Africa
Cyolxauhqui	Mexico

THE MOON IN THE CALENDAR

As time passes, the Moon appears to change shape, from a complete disc (a Full Moon) to a thin slice and back again. Thousands of years ago, the time between one Full Moon and the next was a measure of time. This period is equal to 29.5 days. Ancient Egyptian calendars were based on this time period, which we now call a month. There are roughly 12 New Moons a year, which is why a year has 12 months.

AMAZING FACTS

The traditional stories of many countries include tales about scary things that happen when there's a Full Moon. One example is the changing of a person into a snarling, terrifying wolf, known as a werewolf. This is said to happen in the light of a Full Moon.

In some tales, a person is supposed to turn into a savage half-human, half-wolf known as a werewolf when struck by the light of a Full Moon.

OBSERVING THE MOON

In ancient times, **astronomers** observed and recorded the movement and shape of the Moon. They tried to work out why the Moon appears to move across the sky, how far away it is, and how big it is. Ancient Greek astronomer Hipparchus (about 190–120 BC) was one of the first to think that the Moon was a **sphere**, rather than a flat disc.

A Moon map is vital for any trip to the Moon. You'll need one to find your landing site, and to find your way from crater to crater. Maps are normally divided into the near side (that faces Earth) and the far side (that we never see).

In the book *From the Earth to the Moon*, the author Jules Verne imagined travellers being fired to the Moon inside a giant bullet.

SEEING THE SURFACE

The telescope was invented in the early 1600s. Now astronomers could see the Moon's craters for the first time. As the quality of telescopes improved, they could see more detail, and began to make lunar maps. In the 1800s, the craters got named, mainly in honour of famous astronomers and scientists.

This is one of the detailed sketches of the Moon's surface made by Galileo Galilei, who in the 1600s observed the Moon though a simple telescope.

WHO'S WHO?

Galileo Galilei (1564–1642) was an Italian astronomer, mathematician, and philosopher. In 1609, Galileo heard about a new instrument called a telescope. He worked out how to make his own, and quickly improved the design. He aimed his telescope at the Moon and saw that it is rough and cratered.

LUNAR PROBES

During the 1950s, the United States and the Soviet Union (a group of countries including Russia) began launching robot space probes to the Moon. In 1959, the Soviet *Luna 2* became the first spacecraft to reach the Moon, where it crashed. *Luna 9* was the first spacecraft to land in one piece. It sent the first close-up photographs of the Moon's surface. In the 1960s, US *Surveyor* spacecraft snapped photos of most of the Moon's surface. Later probes brought back rock samples from the Moon.

THE FAR SIDE

The same side of the Moon (called the near side) always faces Earth. From the Earth we can't see the far side. The first-ever pictures of the far side were sent back to Earth by the Soviet probe *Luna 3*, which flew around the Moon in 1959.

The Soviet probe *Lunokhod 1*, which landed on the Moon in 1970, was the first remote-controlled rover to land on another world.

THE LATEST PROBES

Probes from the United States, China, India, and Europe continue to send us information about the Moon. Latest probes include *LRO*, a probe which is mapping the possible landing sites for manned missions, and *GRAIL*, which is helping scientists to work out what's inside the Moon.

AMAZING FACTS

In 2009, **NASA** deliberately crashed a 2-tonne lump of old rocket into the Moon. Following closely behind was a probe called *LCROSS*, which flew through the cloud of **debris** thrown up. Among other things, it found water, confirming that there is some ice on the Moon.

This is what it would have looked like as the *LCROSS* probe approached the Moon.

MOON SCIENCE

Thanks to telescopes, space probes, and **crewed** missions, we have more scientific knowledge about the Moon than about any other body in the **solar system** (except Earth, of course). This knowledge will help you during your Moon mission.

THE MOON, EARTH, AND GRAVITY

The Moon is Earth's **satellite**, and travels around it in a path called an **orbit**. Its orbit is not a perfect circle, so the Moon moves further away from, and closer to, Earth as it orbits. **Gravity** pulls Earth and the Moon together, and this pull keeps the Moon in orbit around Earth.

The Moon's weak gravity means that when you are on the Moon you'll be able to jump much higher than you can on Earth.

Because the Moon is so much smaller than Earth, its gravity is about one-sixth as strong as Earth's. That means an object on the Moon is pulled downwards with only one-sixth of the force as it is on Earth.

MAKING THE MOON

There have been many ideas about where the Moon came from. One idea is that it was captured by Earth's gravity as it drifted by. Today, most astronomers think it was created in a giant space crash. An object about the size of Mars smashed into the young Earth, and rocky material sprayed out into space. This material slowly joined up to form the Moon.

NUMBER CRUNCHING

DIAMETER:
3,476 kilometres (2,160 miles)

MASS (COMPARED TO EARTH):
1.23% of Earth's **mass**

AVERAGE DISTANCE FROM EARTH:
384,400 kilometres (238,855 miles)

AVERAGE SURFACE TEMPERATURE:
−20°Celsius (−4°Fahrenheit)

GRAVITY:
0.17 times Earth gravity

The Moon is much smaller than Earth. The **diameter** of the Moon is just over a quarter of the diameter of Earth.

THE MOON'S PHASES

The Moon seems to change shape from day to day. Sometimes it's a complete disc, sometimes half a disc, and sometimes a thin **crescent**. Why does this happen? The Moon shines because the Sun lights up one side of it. As the Moon orbits Earth, we see different amounts of this lit side. When the Moon is on the same side of Earth as the Sun, we see little or none of the lit side. This is called a New Moon. As the Moon continues in its orbit, more and more of the lit side becomes visible. When the Moon is on the opposite side of Earth to the Sun, we see the whole of the lit side. This is a Full Moon.

What the Moon looks like from Earth

1. new
2. waxing crescent
3. first quarter
4. waxing gibbous
5. full
6. waning gibbous
7. last quarter
8. waning crescent

night time   day time

The Moon's phases happen because different parts of the side of the Moon lit by the Sun are visible from Earth as the Moon orbits.

ECLIPSES

Eclipses happen when Earth, the Moon, and the Sun line up perfectly. A solar eclipse is when the Moon comes between the Sun and Earth, and the Moon's shadow falls on Earth. A lunar eclipse is when Earth's shadow falls on the Moon.

These photographs show how the Moon changes from New Moon to Full Moon and back again over one orbit around the Earth.

NUMBER CRUNCHING

The Moon spins on its **axis** just once on every orbit of Earth (which takes 27.3 days). A place on the Moon gets about two weeks of daylight, then two weeks of darkness. In the day, surface temperatures rise to a roasting 127 degrees Celsius (260 degrees Fahrenheit), and in the night they fall to –173 degrees Celsius (–279 degrees Fahrenheit).

MOON ROCK

The Moon's surface is made entirely of rock and dust. The surface rock has been smashed into pieces over billions of years by numerous **meteorites**. Heating and cooling during the day and night also makes the rock break up. On Earth, in a process called the rock cycle, new rocks are always being made, and old rocks worn away. This doesn't happen on the Moon, so the surface doesn't change.

The Moon's craters range in size from a few centimetres across to hundreds of kilometres across.

SURFACE FEATURES

The Moon's craters were formed by meteorite impacts. The largest craters are called basins. Around the rim of the basins are mountains thousands of metres high. These mountains were formed from the material blasted sideways by the impacts. **Rilles** are deep canyons probably made by flowing lava. The huge dark areas on the Moon are known as *maria* (which means "seas" in Latin), although they contain no water. They were formed when giant craters were flooded by molten rock leaking from under the Moon's crusty outer layer.

There is no **atmosphere** on the Moon. This means that there's no wind or rain to move the dust on the surface around, and tiny craters last forever.

The South Pole-Aitken basin, on the far side of the Moon, is a staggering 2,600 kilometres (1,616 miles) across and more than 8 kilometres (5 miles) deep. It's easily the largest crater on the Moon, and one of the largest in the solar system.

Footprints left in the dust on the Moon are still there because there's no wind to disturb the dust.

INTERVIEW WITH AN ASTRONAUT

Paolo Nespoli is an Italian astronaut with the European Space Agency (ESA). In 2007, Paolo went into space for 15 days, and in 2010 he spent a further 6 months in space. In total, he has orbited Earth an amazing 2,782 times.

Q *Have you always wanted to be an astronaut, since you were a child?*

A Well, this was my childhood dream. When I watched the Apollo astronauts jumping on the Moon and just kind of, you know, bouncing around on the Moon, I thought, when I was a kid, "oh I'd like to be an astronaut!" I was lucky enough to be fascinated as a child by something that later on it turned out that I could accomplish. So, I eventually became an engineer – not because I wanted to be an astronaut or something, it's just because that was what I liked to do. I became an aerospace engineer and every time there was a space selection for an astronaut I would apply and do my best. Eventually I was lucky enough to be selected.

Q *When you're in space, especially on a long trip like you've just come back from, what food do you miss most?*

A In space there is a good amount and quantity of food, but it is very flavoured. This is because in space you tend to lose a little bit of taste, and so they flavour things. There were astronauts that didn't eat because everything tasted like cardboard at the end of the mission, so they are now spicing up the food.

For me, to be honest, I found that after a couple of months, I was missing what I would call in Italy, simply, basic food. You know – spaghetti with tomato sauce. I was terribly missing a pizza. I think I was missing pizza, because I do associate pizza with, you know, going out with friends and being outside and doing things that obviously you cannot do on the space station.

Q *What other daily activities are different when you're travelling in space?*

A We don't really take a shower. We can't take a shower in space because the water goes all over the place, and, by the way, water is a very precious commodity in space and so, for example – people get a little bit astonished – we do actually recycle urine and sweat and we use it again. In space we do keep a good control on the quality of the water, and I'm pretty sure that the water that I drank in space is much safer, much cleaner, much better than what I drink at home, opening up the tap and just drinking from there.

ASTRONAUTS ON THE MOON

Between 1969 and 1972, 12 astronauts of the Apollo space programme landed on the Moon. The programme started after US President John F. Kennedy decided that the United States should try to land men on the Moon. Years of building and testing the Apollo spacecraft and the giant *Saturn V* rocket followed.

AMAZING FACTS

The Apollo spacecraft was designed in the 1960s, only 20 years after computers had first been invented. It had computers to help the astronauts to fly it, but they were less powerful than a modern-day scientific calculator.

A *Saturn V* rocket was a towering 110 metres (361 feet) tall. The Apollo spacecraft fitted into the top part of the rocket.

APOLLO AND SATURN

The Apollo spacecraft was made up of three parts. The first part was the Command Module (CM), where the astronauts travelled. The Service Module (SM) contained a rocket motor and other equipment. The third part, the Lunar Module (LM), actually landed on the Moon. NASA had to build a new rocket, called the *Saturn V,* to launch this heavy spacecraft into space.

Apollo spacecraft made several test missions before the first landing. In late 1968, *Apollo 8* carried astronauts on the first manned trip around the Moon. *Apollo 9* tested the Lunar Module in Earth orbit, and *Apollo 10* astronauts practised a trip to the Moon, but didn't land.

Lunar Module   Command Module   Service Module

This diagram shows the three sections of the Apollo spacecraft.

FIRST PEOPLE ON THE MOON

On 16 July 1969, *Apollo 11* took off from the Kennedy Space Centre in Florida, USA. On board was a crew of three astronauts: Neil Armstrong (the commander), Buzz Aldrin, and Michael Collins. Just over three days later, *Apollo 11* settled into orbit around the Moon. The next day Armstrong and Aldrin climbed into the Lunar Module and descended to the surface, leaving Collins in charge of the Command Module.

WHO'S WHO?

Edwin "Buzz" Aldrin (born 1930) was a fighter pilot in the US Air Force. He started training as an astronaut in 1963, and made his first space flight in 1966 aboard *Gemini 12*. Three years later, he was chosen as a member of the crew of *Apollo 11*, and became the second person to stand on the Moon.

Michael Collins took this photograph of *Apollo 11*'s Lunar Module with Neil Armstrong and Buzz Aldrin aboard, just after they undocked from the Command Module.

Armstrong and Aldrin set up scientific instruments on the surface, gathered samples of dust and rock to take back to Earth, and raised a US flag.

A GIANT STEP

Apollo 11's Lunar Module, named *Eagle*, landed in the Sea of Tranquillity (one of the Moon's *maria*). A few hours later Armstrong climbed down the ladder and jumped onto the Moon's surface. Aldrin soon followed. After just 21 hours on the Moon, Armstrong and Aldrin rejoined Collins in orbit.

AMAZING FACTS

The flight computer on *Apollo 11*'s Lunar Module tried to land Armstrong and Aldrin in a field of giant boulders. Armstrong quickly took over control. Using precious fuel, he flew over the boulders, then a crater, before touching down. There was just 30 seconds worth of fuel left.

RETURN TO THE MOON

Six more Apollo missions followed on the success of *Apollo 11*. Each mission (except *Apollo 13* – see panel) visited a different area of the Moon. Each time the astronauts stayed a little longer on the surface. The astronauts set up numerous experiments to find out more about the Moon, and took thousands of photographs. In total, they brought 382 kilograms (842 pounds) of Moon rock back to Earth. They even had time for fun – *Apollo 14* astronaut Alan Shepard hit a golf shot on the Moon!

FINAL MISSION

Apollo 17 was the final Apollo mission. Astronauts Eugene Cernan and Harrison Schmitt stayed on the Moon's surface for nearly three Earth days. They left on 14 December 1972, with Cernan the last man to leave the surface. Nobody has been to the Moon since.

AMAZING FACTS

As *Apollo 13* travelled towards the Moon, an **oxygen** tank in the Service Module exploded and damaged the spacecraft. The astronauts were left short of oxygen to breathe, and they were in serious danger. They used the oxygen in the lunar module, but were lucky to get back to Earth alive.

You might want to take a hammer and a feather to the Moon. Why? To recreate a famous experiment. *Apollo 15* astronaut Dave Scott dropped a hammer and a feather from the same height above the surface. Both hit the surface at the same time, just as Galileo had predicted hundreds of years earlier, based on the laws of motion.

The astronauts of *Apollo 15*, *Apollo 16*, and *Apollo 17* explored the Lunar surface in a battery-powered Lunar Roving Vehicle (LRV).

PLANNING A MOON MISSION

A mission to the Moon needs extremely careful planning. When will you go? Who will go with you? Where will you land? What kit will you take? Once that rocket blasts off there's no going back! You could be away for more than a week, in a very **hostile** environment, nothing like the cosy Earth that you'll be leaving behind.

NASA's Multi-Purpose Crew Vehicle is being developed. As well as travelling to the International Space Station, it may one day carry humans to Mars or to an asteroid.

SPACECRAFT AND ROCKET

Any spacecraft that takes you to the Moon must carry you and all your equipment, but also do many other jobs for you. The spacecraft will need a powerful rocket to lift it away from Earth's gravity. It must protect you from dangerous **radiation** from the Sun and from space, keep you warm, and provide air for you to breathe. It must also land safely on the Moon. On the return journey, it must protect you from the immense heat of re-entry to Earth's atmosphere.

During lift-off from the launch pad, the rocket will increase speed so fast that you'll be pressed right down into your seat. You will feel as if your body is four or five times as heavy as normal! This uncomfortable feeling only lasts a few minutes, until the spacecraft is in Earth's orbit. When the rocket motors turn off, you'll feel completely weightless.

Modern rockets, such as the *Ariane 5*, are often used to take satellites into orbit around Earth.

WHO'S GOING WITH YOU?

Who would your ideal travelling companions be? Here are some useful people you might want to come along for the ride.

CREW MEMBER:

NEIL ARMSTRONG (BORN 1930)

Neil Armstrong was an American fighter pilot and **test pilot** before joining NASA to train as an astronaut in 1962. In 1969, he was chosen as commander of the *Apollo 11* mission, and became the first person to stand on the Moon.

POTENTIAL JOB:

mission commander

CREW MEMBER:

ISAAC NEWTON (1642–1727)

Isaac Newton was an English professor of mathematics at Cambridge University. He was the first scientist to realize that things fall to the ground because of gravity. In 1687, he published *Mathematical Principles of Natural Philosophy*, which describes how gravity controls the movement of all objects in space.

POTENTIAL JOB:

mission scientist

CREW MEMBER:

JULES VERNE (1828–1905)

In his thirties, French science-fiction writer Jules Verne quit his job to become a full-time writer. Over the next 40 years, he wrote dozens of science-fiction stories. One his most famous stories is *From the Earth to the Moon*, written in 1865.

POTENTIAL JOB:

to write the mission diary

CREW MEMBER:

SALLY RIDE (BORN 1951)

US scientist Sally Ride was chosen by NASA to train as an astronaut in 1978. On 18 June 1983, she went into space on board the space shuttle *Challenger*. She has written several children's books about being an astronaut.

POTENTIAL JOB:

astronaut

CREW MEMBER:

JEAN-MICHEL COUSTEAU (BORN 1938)

Jean-Michel Cousteau is the son of the famous Jacques Cousteau, inventor of SCUBA diving equipment. He has explored and made films about the oceans. He is also an environmentalist, trying to protect the oceans.

POTENTIAL JOB:

expert on breathing equipment

WHAT TO TAKE

On a mission to the Moon, you can take some personal equipment, but there will be a strict weight limit (it was just 2 kilograms (5 pounds) each on the Apollo missions). So you might have some tricky choices to make. You might want to take a media player (with music, photos from home, and books). But forget your mobile phone – there won't be a signal in space!

SUITED UP

You'll need to put on a spacesuit whenever you leave your spacecraft to explore the surface of the Moon. This is probably the most complicated and expensive suit you'll ever wear! Its many layers protect you from the Sun's heat and from high-speed micrometeorites. It will provide you with oxygen to breathe and keep you warm.

Astronauts performing "spacewalks" outside the International Space Station wear the sort of spacesuits that you would wear on the surface of the Moon.

FOOD AND DRINK

Some food and drink will be **dehydrated** – you can just add water and heat them up. Other food will be in tins or pouches. Only a small tank of water is carried on a spacecraft. Water is a **byproduct** of the spacecraft's **fuel cells** (which are like batteries). Water is also recycled – water vapour from your breath is removed from the air, and is also extracted (taken) from urine. But don't worry, it's probably cleaner than water from your tap on Earth!

DON'T FORGET

What memento or lucky charm would you carry with you on a Moon mission? Neil Armstrong (commander of *Apollo 11*) carried a piece of wood from a propeller of the Wright Brothers' 1903 aeroplane.

This is food for astronauts on the International Space Station, including creamed spinach and sugar-coated peanuts. It is dehydrated to save weight and space.

SIGHTS TO SEE ON THE MOON

There are plenty of amazing sights to see on the Moon. You might be able to see some of these as your spacecraft orbits the Moon.

Tycho crater

Tycho is a ray crater, which means the rock that was thrown up by the impact is visible in lines or "rays" of light-coloured rock leading away from the crater. Tycho's rays are visible from Earth during a Full Moon.

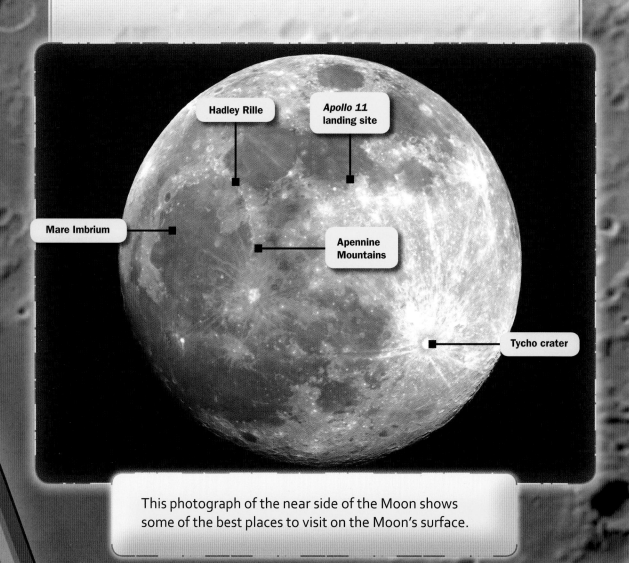

Hadley Rille

Apollo 11 landing site

Mare Imbrium

Apennine Mountains

Tycho crater

This photograph of the near side of the Moon shows some of the best places to visit on the Moon's surface.

Mare Imbrium

The Mare Imbrium is the largest of the Moon's seas, measuring a vast 1,200 kilometres (750 miles) across. The Mare Imbrium is surrounded by mountain chains. Mare Imbrium means "Sea of Rains", but it is actually completely dry.

Apennine Mountains

The Apennine mountain range is 600 kilometres (373 miles) long and up to 5 kilometres (3 miles) high on the edge of the Mare Imbrium (see above), thrown up when the Mare Imbrium was formed by a giant impact.

Hadley Rille

The Hadley Rille is a valley 135 kilometres (84 miles) long, 1–2 kilometres (0.6–1.2 miles) wide, and 370 metres (1,214 feet) deep.

Apollo 11 landing site

Visit this historic site on the edge of the Sea of Tranquillity to see the footprints of Neil Armstrong and Buzz Aldrin, the lower section of *Eagle*, their Lunar Lander, and all the kit they left behind.

DON'T FORGET

As your spacecraft orbits the Moon before landing, watch out for Earth coming up over the Moon's **horizon** – just as you can see the Moon rise from Earth.

INTERVIEW WITH A SPACE SCIENTIST

John Spencer is a NASA scientist. He works mainly on the Cassini mission, which is exploring the moons of Saturn, as well as Saturn itself. His team plans where *Cassini* spacecraft will go and what information it will gather.

Q *Do you think we will ever have human colonies in space?*

A I think it's possible, but it's only possible if we can make space travel a lot cheaper than it is now. To get a colony where six people can live on the International Space Station – we can barely afford that. It's going to be a long way in the future, I think. It's certainly not the way I thought it would be when I was 12 years old watching the Apollo astronauts on the Moon and imagining that by now we would have huge space colonies and people would be exploring the moons of Jupiter.

Q *Do you have any space heroes?*

A People like Eugene Shoemaker who was a geologist, and who was one of the first people to get interested in impact craters and to understand how you can learn about craters on the Moon by studying craters on Earth. He was one of the first people to really figure out the geology of the Moon. It was amazing what he did and I was privileged enough to get to know him.

My original inspiration was those Apollo astronauts going off and walking on the surface of the Moon. It blew my mind when I was a kid that it was possible for people to do that, just to imagine them being so far away. I was just old enough to really get it, how amazing it was.

Q *Why do you think it is important that we study space?*

A Well, you know, you can spend your life in your house, or you can get out and get to know your neighbourhood. And that's what we're doing. We're just learning amazing things about our own planet as we do so. For example, we see all these craters on the Moon, and once we realized that those weren't volcanoes, those were produced by things smashing in to the Moon, then you realize that, well, that must have happened to Earth as well. So, that really changes how you think about the history of Earth. Earth was pummelled early in its history and would have been covered in craters in the way the Moon is, and no one would have thought of that if we hadn't gone and explored and figured out what all these holes in the ground on the Moon were.

ON THE MOON

The Moon's surface is a hostile environment. Remember that there's no atmosphere, and it can be roasting hot or freezing cold. You'll spend most of your time inside your spacecraft, perhaps doing some science experiments, and eating and sleeping. When you go outside to walk across the dusty surface – this is called an extra-vehicular activity (EVA) – you'll have to put on your spacesuit.

A SHORT STAY

All the basic things you take for granted at home will be missing on the Moon. That includes air to breathe, water to drink, and food to eat. Electricity will come from **solar panels** and fuel cells, so the supply is limited. This means that you can't stay on the Moon for more than a few days before returning, otherwise supplies will begin to run out.

DON'T FORGET

Harmful rays from the Sun and from space hit the Moon all the time. You'll have to wear a device called a dosimeter, which measures how much radiation has hit you during your time outside. If your dose gets too high, you'll have to stay inside your spaceship.

WHEN TO VISIT

Whatever your destination on the Moon, don't forget that there will be about two weeks of daylight, followed by two weeks of darkness. So choose your landing spot in a place where it will be daytime. Otherwise you'll see nothing, your solar panels won't work, and it will be extremely cold. Any time of year will be fine, because there are no seasons on the Moon.

You'll want to take plenty of snapshots of the Moon. Here is *Apollo* astronaut Richard Gordon taking photos of the Moon from the Command Module of *Apollo* 12, in 1969.

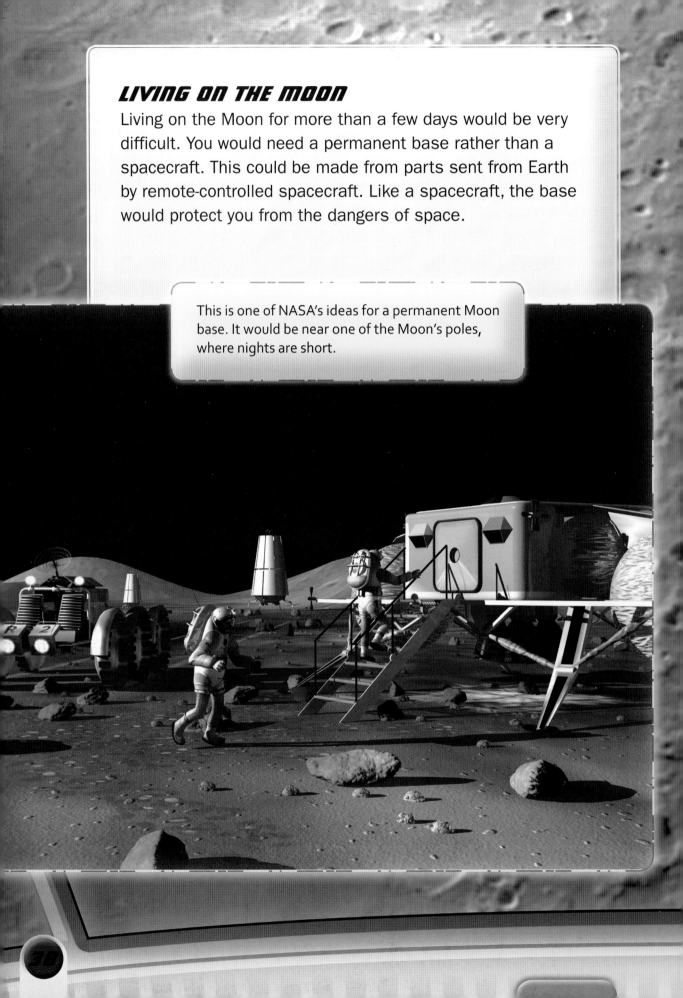

LIVING ON THE MOON

Living on the Moon for more than a few days would be very difficult. You would need a permanent base rather than a spacecraft. This could be made from parts sent from Earth by remote-controlled spacecraft. Like a spacecraft, the base would protect you from the dangers of space.

This is one of NASA's ideas for a permanent Moon base. It would be near one of the Moon's poles, where nights are short.

For a long stay on the Moon, you would need to make use of Moon materials. Ice has been found near the Moon's poles, and this could be collected for water. Water is made up of hydrogen and oxygen, so the oxygen could be taken out and used to breathe. A base would probably be set up at one of the Moon's poles, where there's permanent sunlight to run solar panels for electricity. Food could be supplied from Earth at first, but then it would need to be grown in special greenhouses.

RETURN TO THE MOON

Several countries around the world have plans to send astronauts to the Moon in the future, but there are no definite dates yet. Getting to the Moon is a very complex and hugely expensive task, and it will probably be 2025 at the earliest before astronauts land there again. It will be many more years before any sort of Moon base is established.

AMAZING FACTS

The European Space Agency is taking a new approach to Moon exploration. It is experimenting with a robot astronaut called Justin, which is being tested on the International Space Station. Justin could eventually visit the Moon instead of human astronauts.

MAP OF THE SOLAR SYSTEM

MERCURY

VENUS

EARTH

MARS

ASTEROID BELT

JUPITER

SATURN

URANUS

NEPTUNE

The sizes of the planets and their distances from the Sun are not to scale. To show all the planets' real distances from the Sun, this page would have to be about one kilometre long!

TIMELINE

100s BC
Ancient Greek astronomer Hipparchusis is one of the first people to decide that the Moon is a sphere.

1600s
The invention of the telescope allows astronomers such as Galileo Galilei to see the Moon's surface in detail for the first time.

1959
The space probe *Luna 2* is the first spacecraft to reach the Moon, where it crashes.
Luna 3 sends pictures of the far side of the Moon back to Earth.

1962
US President John F. Kennedy announces that the United States plans to send astronauts to the Moon by 1970.

1966
Luna 9 is the first probe to land on the Moon.

1968
Apollo 8 carries astronauts around the Moon for the first time.

1969
Apollo 11 lands on the Moon with astronauts Neil Armstrong and Buzz Aldrin.

1970
Apollo 13 returns safely to Earth after an explosion on board on the way to the Moon.

1972
Astronauts of *Apollo 17* visit the Moon. No astronauts have been to the Moon since.

2009
The probe *LCROSS* flies into a cloud of dust thrown up by deliberately crashing an old rocket into the Moon's surface.

FACT FILE

DIAMETER:
3,476 kilometres
(2,160 miles)

AVERAGE DISTANCE FROM EARTH:
384,400 kilometres
(238,855 miles)

SMALLEST DISTANCE FROM EARTH:
356,410 kilometres
(221,463 miles)

FURTHEST DISTANCE FROM EARTH:
406,697 kilometres
(252,710 miles)

TIME FOR ONE ORBIT OF EARTH:
27 Earth days, 7 hours, 43 minutes

DAY LENGTH:
29 Earth days, 12 hours, 44 minutes

AVERAGE SURFACE TEMPERATURE:
−20°C (−4°F)

HIGHEST SURFACE TEMPERATURE:
127°C (260°F)

LOWEST SURFACE TEMPERATURE:
−173°C (−279°F)

GRAVITY:
0.17 times Earth gravity

LARGEST CRATER:
South Pole–Aitken Basin, diameter 2,600 kilometres (1,616 miles)

FIRST SPACE PROBE TO CRASH ONTO THE MOON:
Luna 2 (1959)

FIRST SPACECRAFT TO LAND ON THE MOON:
Luna 9 (1966)

FIRST LUNAR ROVER:
Lunokhod 1 (1970)

FIRST ASTRONAUTS ON THE MOON:
Neil Armstrong and Buzz Aldrin, *Apollo 11* (1969)

GLOSSARY

astronomer person who studies space

atmosphere layer of gases surrounding a planet

axis line through a planet or moon that the planet or moon spins round. It always goes through the planet or moon's poles.

byproduct useful product that is made during the manufacture of another product

canyon valley with very steep or vertical sides

crater dish-shaped hole in the surface of a planet, made by a meteorite smashing into the surface

crescent curved shape with two pointed ends

crewed spacecraft that has people on board

debris loose material, such as small pieces of broken rock

dehydrated dried out

diameter distance from one side of a circle or sphere to the other

fuel cell device that makes electricity by mixing two chemicals (such as oxygen and hydrogen)

gravity force that pulls objects towards each other. Big objects, such as planets, have much stronger gravity than smaller objects, such as people.

horizon the line between the ground (or sea) and the sky

hostile unfriendly and dangerous

lava molten rock that flows on the surface of a planet

lunar to do with the Moon

maria huge dark areas on the Moon (the word means "seas" in Latin)

mass measure of the amount of material that makes up an object

meteorite piece of rock from space that hits the surface of a planet or moon

NASA National Aeronautics and Space Administration, the US space agency

orbit path of a planet or other satellite around a larger body, such as the Sun

oxygen gas that we need to breathe to stay alive, and one of the gases in Earth's atmosphere

probe robot spacecraft sent to visit planets, moons, and other objects in the solar system

radiation particles and rays that come from some objects in space, such as stars. Some types of radiation are harmful to humans.

rille narrow channel or canyon in the surface of a planet or Moon

satellite object, often human-made, that orbits a larger object

solar panel device that makes electricity from sunlight

solar system the Sun, the planets that orbit around the Sun, their moons, and other objects that orbit the Sun, such as asteroids and comets

sphere perfectly round ball-shaped object

telescope device that makes distant objects look bigger

test pilot pilot who flies new types of aircraft to make sure they work properly

FIND OUT MORE

BOOKS

Exploring the Moon (Space Guides), Peter Grego
  (QED, 2007)

The Earth and its Moon, Chris Oxlade (Wayland, 2007)

Moon, Stewart Ross (Oxford University Press, 2009)

The Moon (True Books), Elaine Landau (Children's
  Press, 2008)

Space Detectives' Handbook, Sue Becklake
  (Miles Kelly, 2009)

Wow! Space (Dorling Kindersley, 2010)

WEBSITES

astro.unl.edu/naap/lps/animations/lps.swf
This interactive diagram shows why we see phases of
the Moon.

www.esa.int/esaKIDSen
Learn more about life in space and what the European
Space Agency does on their children's web pages.

www.nasa.gov/missions/past/index.html
Learn more about past, present, and future NASA missions.

solarsystem.nasa.gov/timeline/index.html
See who has explored space before you with this timeline.

school.discoveryeducation.com/schooladventures/skywatch
Find out what a fab hobby watching the sky at night can be.

DVDS

Apollo 13 (Universal Pictures, 1995)
The Apollo Missions (Pegasus Entertainments, 2009)
The Planets (BBC Worldwide, 2000)

PLACES TO VISIT

The National Space Centre
Exploration Drive, Leicester LE4 5NS
www.spacecentre.co.uk

Science Museum
Exhibition Road, South Kensington, London SW7 4DD
www.sciencemuseum.org.uk

Spaceport
Victoria Place, Seacombe, Wallasey, Wirral CH44 6QY
www.spaceport.org.uk

FURTHER RESEARCH

Here are some starting points for finding out more about the Moon:

- Look at the Moon in the night sky, with the naked eye and through binoculars. Try to identify some of the seas and craters with the help of a Moon map.
- Research some of the ideas about how the Moon was made.
- Look at images and videos of solar and lunar eclipses.
- Follow the progress of the latest missions of probes to the Moon.
- Find out about living in zero gravity.
- Find out more about the story of *Apollo 13*.

INDEX